The Leader As Coach

HOW TO COACH A WINNING TEAM

By
Richard C. Huseman, Ph.D.

Equity Press

Library of Congress Cataloging-in-Publication Data

Relational Intelligence (RQ) is copyrighted by
Richard C. Huseman, Ph.D.

The Coaching Scorecard is copyrighted by
Richard C. Huseman, Ph.D.

Huseman, Richard C.
The leader as coach: How to coach a winning team
Richard C. Huseman
p.   cm.

ISBN: 0-9712260-2-4
1. Leadership   2. Coaching   3. Fairness
4. Interpersonal relations   5. Employee Motivation – United States

Printed in the United States of America

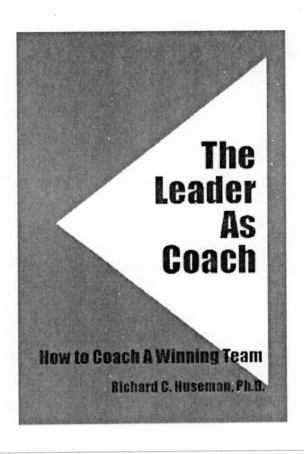

To learn more about **The Leader As Coach** and related workshops, seminars, training programs, leadership assessment instruments, quantity discounts for this and other publications, or to contact Dr. Huseman, please visit www.give-to-get.com

Dedicated to

Coach Thomas "Pix" Bowerman

My high school basketball, baseball and track coach

Pix never made big money,
but he did make a big difference
…in my life and the lives of many others.

Thanks, Pix.

ACKNOWLEDGEMENTS

For the last 30 years, it has been my good fortune to work with leaders in a wide variety of organizations. Some of those leaders were in Fortune 50 companies; others were start-up entrepreneurs. They included both public and private organizations. Needless to say, I have seen a broad spectrum of leadership styles. In my early years, command and control was the predominant approach – in many organizations today, it still is. But, as enlightened leaders have come to realize that their success depends less and less on physical and financial assets and more and more on human assets – I have also seen a major evolution in leadership style.

There are many descriptions you could use to describe how these enlightened leaders lead – whether they are CEO's or front line supervisors. For me, one term captures best what these enlightened leaders do – they coach.

I have had the opportunity to observe many of these "coaches" practice their craft. Many of those coaching practices have had their impact on this little book and I want to acknowledge all of their contributions – and they know who they are even though the sheer number of them doesn't permit an individual listing of names.

Zulema Seguel has provided suggestions, ideas, editorial support and at key times, offered "coaching." Thanks, Zu.

THE COACHING MAP

4. Coaching Your Winning Team 31

FOREWORD

The health care industry is one of dynamic and rapid change. Time is short, the challenges numerous and the opportunities great. To keep us at our best both spiritually and financially, we must be able to adapt to change while holding strongly to our core values – as individuals and as an organization.

In my ongoing search for ways to enhance our core values of Integrity, Care, Balance, Excellence, Stewardship and Teamwork, I have become aware of a powerful tool for enhancing these qualities at every level of Florida Hospital. What is this tool? The tool is COACHING. By shifting from "managing" to "coaching" at every level of the organization, we can foster a culture that allows both individuals and the organization to thrive.

I have recently seen the power and potential coaching can have for individuals and teams. *Having* a coach gives you the feedback and motivation to play at the top of your game. *Being* a coach allows you to provide feedback and serve in a supportive role helping others to reach their peak performance.

This is why I chose to write a foreword to this book, **The Leader As Coach: How To Lead A Winning Team**. The ideas and practices laid out in this book promote that we all work together to inspire growth – for the organization and for ourselves. It shows us how we can coach each other to stretch our limits and maximize our potential so that we all play at our best... with all of our heart and spirit. As we coach others in their growth and development, something interesting happens. We grow and develop ourselves. In a healthy coaching relationship, both participants benefit so that we all play with more enthusiasm, strength and commitment.

I believe that by engaging in a coaching approach, we can help each other enhance our skill to heal and our spirit to care.

I offer this book as a way to enhance your relationship with Florida Hospital and with your fellow teammates. After reading this book, I am sure you, too, will want to make the simple, powerful shift to a coaching mindset. It will open a whole new world of growth, high performance and caring for others. I know it has for me.

Lars Houmann
Executive Vice President
Chief Operating Officer
Florida Hospital

Chapter 1

The New Importance of Leadership

Regardless of your title – CEO, manager, supervisor, coordinator, etc. – if you have people reporting to you on a daily basis, then you *are a leader*.

In organizations today, decisions are being pushed down to the lowest possible levels so they'll get made and get made quickly. No matter where you stand in the corporate hierarchy, you no longer have the luxury of facing a problem and waiting for someone else at the top to solve it for you.

In order to be successful, you must be willing to make quick decisions, negotiate deals, structure work assignments, and grab opportunities when they appear before you. To do this, you will very much need the help of the people who report directly to you. And if those people aren't loyal to you, then you're toast.

The Concept Of Corporate Loyalty

In the old days, people might not have liked their immediate manager. In fact, they might have even loathed him or her. But those employees could count on working 10, 15, 20+ years with the same company and in addition to getting a reasonable paycheck, they had the confidence of knowing that their jobs (and futures) were safe and secure.

That security encouraged many employees to put up with inept or surly managers. The hassle of having to deal with sub-par leadership day-to-day in exchange for job security and a good pension for the retirement years was worth the tradeoff. So, most employees remained loyal to the company, no matter what they thought of their immediate manager.

The Demise Of Corporate Loyalty

But corporate loyalty is hard to find these days. Why? Too often in recent years, employees have been left holding the short end of the stick in their relationships with their employers. They find themselves doing more and more work, and making more and more sacrifices, with little or no return for their efforts.

Worse yet, many employees have seen their years of hard work and commitment count for nothing as they lost their jobs during an era of downsizing and merger. Even if your organization has escaped the downsizing ax, the media has made sure we all know about – and fear – the slash and burn strategies that are a part of business today. In this kind of business environment, people find it hard to develop strong trusting relationships with their companies.

The New Importance of Leadership

The New Loyalty Contract

So, with whom can employees build loyal and trusting relationships with? It's someone they see often and work with day-to-day – their immediate leader.

Yes, we mean you! You have now become the focal point for how people think and feel about their jobs and how well (or poorly) they decide to do them.

- **The number one reason people say they *quit* their jobs is their immediate manager.**

- **But, on a positive note, the number one reason people say they *stay, work hard and like* their jobs is, again, their immediate manager.**

If you, as a manager/leader, don't have solid working relationships with the people who report to you, then you won't have their loyalty or full cooperation. You have to be able to depend on them and the effort they're willing to give you in order to help you make decisions and get the job done right. If you have only their heads and not their hearts – if you can't capture their willingness to give you everything they've got – then you aren't being an effective leader in today's work environment. And, one way or another, you'll end up paying a very hefty price for your lack of leadership.

If you are not a good leader –
be prepared to pay the price for your lack of leadership.

The Importance of Trust

Trust, of course, is important in all relationships, but it's especially crucial between you and the people who report to you. If you don't have it, you're going to get nowhere fast. Several years ago, researchers at The Center for Creative Leadership identified the chief causes business executives fail in their organizations. At the very top of their list were arrogance and insensitivity to other people. Running a very close second was not being trustworthy.

Are you trustworthy? If you are like most people, based on a scale from 1 to 10 (10 being the most trustworthy), odds are that you consider yourself to be between a 7 or an 8. Now, using that same scale, as a whole, how trustworthy do you consider other people to be? The typical responses we hear to this question are 4, 5, or 6.

How does this relate to your job? A survey by researchers at Boston University found that 80% of employees in organizations simply don't trust top management.

Why? Well, let's start with some of your own biases. Assume that you believe that trustworthy people tell the truth and keep their word. Now make a mental list of occupations you see as being untrustworthy. How about used car salespersons? Mechanics? Politicians? Journalists? Lawyers? Given a little time, you probably could fill out a very long list. One reason we have trouble trusting others is our assumption is that they will take advantage of us, lie to us, cheat and steal from us, in order to get what they want from a relationship.

Another reason trusting others is difficult is that trust in relationships does not come about quickly. When beginning a new relationship, we tend to withhold trust until others prove that they can be trusted. People have to earn our trust just like they have to earn our respect and friendship. New employees are less likely to be given access to confidential company information than are senior employees who have already justified our confidence in them. Thus we refuse to trust other people who simply say, "Trust me." Our position is, "Show me first that you can be trusted!"

The final problem is that trust is very fragile, like a piece of fine china. Building a relationship based on trust can take a very long time, but smashing it can take only seconds. One simple violation of trust shatters whatever trust has been built, and we then suspect that the person can't be trusted at all, ever. Once our trust has been violated, we usually aren't willing to give that person a second chance. If we do, we do it very grudgingly.

So, how can you build and maintain trusting relationships with others at work? Trust, like all human attributes, is based primarily on perceptions not necessarily reality. There are three essential qualities in a work-oriented relationship on which trust is constructed:

- How competent people think you are.

- How caring people think you are about others.

- How dependable people think you are in being both caring and competent over time.

Depending on how people perceive your combination of competence and caring, you may find yourself in one of four types of trust relationships:

- Relationships based primarily on Respect

- Relationships based primarily on Affection

- Relationships in Trust Bankruptcy

- Relationships based on High Trust

Here is a guide to each one of these types of trust relationships.

Building Trust

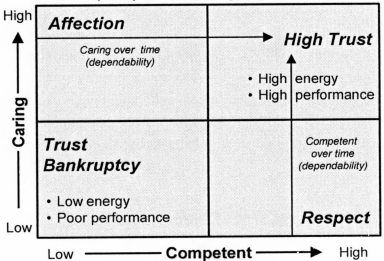

Relationships Based On Respect: If people see you as being very competent at your job but caring little or not at all about people, you probably will earn the respect of those around you, but not their trust. Many of us have known people who are great at their jobs, but whose attitude toward people is so cold and indifferent that we would trust them only as far as we could throw them.

Relationships Based On Affection: If you are perceived as highly caring of others, but not perceived as very competent at what you do, those you work with may think of you affectionately as a friend or a kind person, but they won't necessarily think enough of your judgment to consider you much of a leader.

Relationships In Trust Bankruptcy: If the people who work for you don't see you as being either caring or competent (as many now see their organizations, thanks to the era of downsizing and merger), then your relationship with them is in trust bankruptcy. As a leader, your effectiveness in your relationships with the people who work for you is at great risk because there is simply no foundation on which to base the relationship.

Relationships Based On High Trust: If you are perceived by people to be both highly competent at your job and genuinely caring about people – and you are able to demonstrate these two qualities again and again over time (i.e., you are perceived as dependable), then you are well on your way to building high trust relationships with your employees. As a leader, high trust relationships are the foundation to fostering high performance work relationships.

So, with the old loyalty contract with the organization now null and void, you, as your employee's immediate leader, are the key to getting their loyalty and trust. If you want your people to "stay, work hard and like" their jobs, you need to be seen as both caring and competent over time. How? The secret is in how you choose to lead your team.

The Coaching Test

As a leader, there are several approaches you can take to how you lead people. For starters, let's take the following test: Check one:

- ☐ I want to be "managed"
- ☐ I want to be "coached"

If you checked you want to be managed, put down this book and go do something else. If you checked you want to be coached, keep reading... because chances are, members of your team want to be coached, too. And, coaching is the key to getting the trust and performance you need to lead a winning team.

The Leader As Coach

Chapter 2

The Leader As Coach

Since you are still reading, you obviously decided you didn't want to be "managed" – you wanted to be coached. So do most people, including those that work for you. What's the difference? Why does being "coached" sound so much more appealing then being "managed?"

> *If you want to be an effective coach in business –*
> *think about what an athletic coach does.*

In order to answer that question, let's look at what comes to mind when we think of an athletic team coach. What does a coach do that makes most of us as players want to be coached?

- Coaches have a nose for talent that fits the culture of the team.

- Coaches have a bold vision that affirms the team can win and how they will win.

- Coaches tap our desire to win.

- Coaches help us perform to the best of our ability.

- Coaches help us build on our strengths and help us manage our weaknesses.

- Coaches know how to motivate us – both as a team and individually.

- Coaches give us feedback, feedback, feedback.

- Coaches are great storytellers.

- Coaches know how important it is to celebrate… even the small wins.

Lessons From Coach Pix

For me, I was lucky early on in my life to see first hand what a great coach can do. I grew up and went to school in a small town called Alamo in central Indiana. The school was set up so that grades 1-6 were located on the first floor and grades 7-12 were housed in one large room on the second floor (like I said, it was a small town and admittedly a rather long time ago). All grades shared the "state of the art" gym that was built for one main purpose – basketball.

The Leader As Coach

Our coach at the time was a man by the name of Thomas "Pix" Bowerman and he was the basketball coach during my entire 12-years of schooling at Alamo. From the day I started 1st grade, I knew about Pix and the major role he played at the school. When it came to town notoriety, the principal had nothing on Pix. You see, in Alamo, basketball was the main Friday night social event and, as coach, Pix ran the show.

Coach Pix was a living example of
what great coaches do to help their teams win.

If you want a better picture of what it was like, just think about the movie "Hoosiers" and you'll be right on the money. That's what it was like in Alamo when I was growing up.

Pix was a living example of what great coaches do to help their teams win. I remember he scoped out talent early, showing up during 4th, 5th, and 6th grade recess and showing us how to shoot, how to dribble the ball with either hand, and especially how to shoot free throws. Pix looked for kids that would be a fit for the team he had built up… kids who didn't smoke, didn't drink, and kids he thought would be team players.

When I was in the 7th and 8th grade, we started to play teams from other schools. I was definitely not the "star" of our team – that honor belonged to a boy named Carl. Carl was 6 to 10 inches taller and considerably stronger than most other guys on the team and he dominated rebounds. From his size alone, Carl was a guy a coach could build a championship team around – 6 feet 1 inch tall in the 8th grade. We only had a couple of *seniors* that were 6'2" or 6'3", so you can imagine the potential of having an eighth grader already that tall with a growth spurt or more to go.

Everyone thought that by the time Carl was a senior, he would be the star player on a team that would win the county championship. In all of his years of coaching, Pix had never won the championship but he was convinced that our group – with the help of Carl – could do it.

Even as eighth graders, Pix was already talking to us about what it would be like to win the county championship when we were juniors or seniors. He was always sharing stories about great teams and great players of the past at Alamo. It was clear to all of us that Carl would be one of these great players and a major part of that potential championship team. You can imagine how we all felt the day during my freshman year when Coach Pix announced before practice that Carl was no longer on the team.

Wow!

You could have heard a pin drop as the whole team looked at Coach Pix in disbelief. Carl was out? We had all heard rumors that Carl didn't always follow the rules Coach Pix had for his players. Carl smoked and was known to drink (which was pretty unusual at that time for a freshman). What we didn't

The Leader As Coach

know was that Coach Pix had given Carl a couple of strong warnings to shape up and clean up his act. But, after Carl had had some run-ins with the police, Coach Pix decided to put Carl off the team… permanently.

It couldn't have been an easy decision. Carl, who played center, had been the crux of our entire strategy to get to the county championships. Not only that, but Coach Pix knew that the rest of us on the team had banked on Carl as well. The team was going to be hard pressed to believe that they could still win without Carl.

But, Coach Pix didn't miss a beat. He immediately changed our usual routine and had us working more on perimeter shooting, more practice at free throws, etc. At the end of practice, he pulled us aside and told us that, even without Carl, we were still going to win the county championships when we were juniors or seniors. We didn't know how. Looking back, I'm not sure Pix knew either. But, he did know that he had to get us to believe we could win, Carl or no Carl.

▶▶ Fast-forward four years… ▶▶

My senior year, the Alamo Warriors, as one of ten competing teams, won the Montgomery County Basketball Championship. With trophy in hand, the entire team climbed onto the Alamo Volunteer Fire Truck and drove up and down the streets of Alamo with sirens blaring and lights flashing to celebrate the fact that we were the county champs.

Looking back at my experiences with Coach Pix, he was a great coach. Go back to the list of what great coaches do. He tapped our desire to win, he tapped our desire to play at the top of our ability, he hit every one of the items on the list right on the head.

But, I think his greatest skill was knowing when a player did not fit the culture he established for the team. Pix had the foresight to "see" that Carl and his behavior were not a fit for the team – no matter how much talent the kid had. I can only imagine what would have happened had Pix tolerated Carl's behavior and then, sometime later down the line, been forced to take him off the team. As it turned out, Carl dropped out of school in his junior year. As a team, if we had still been depending on Carl then, we could never have won the championship.

Do you "manage" or "coach" your team?

Do You "Manage" Or Do You "Coach?"

Now, what about you? Do you think you currently "manage" or "coach" your team? Unless you can look at the list of what great athletic coaches do and can say you do pretty much the same thing with your team, chances are you are more of a "manager" than a "coach."

The Leader As Coach

How do you think your team feels about being "managed?" If you think that there's a good chance they would be happier and more productive if they were "coached," start working with the list and keep reading. The difference between managing and coaching is basically one of perspective – namely *yours*. It just takes a simple shift in how you see your role as a leader. And we are going to show you how to make this shift.

The Leader As Coach

Chapter 3

What A Coach Really Does:

Getting You From Where You Are

To Where You Want To Be

In the 1500's in England, "a coach" referred to a particular type of carriage. "To be coached," meant to carry a person from where they were to where they wanted to be. So it is in the world of coaching today. As a coach, you can help your team and individuals on that team get from where they are to where they want to be.

Now, be very careful and look at this sentence again.

> As a coach, you can help your team get from
> where they are to where *they want to be* –
> not where *you want them to be*.

As a coach, you can have major influence on your team and the individuals that make up that team. As a coach, you can also have influence on the desirability of attaining a certain goal or level of performance. But, the team you are coaching (and the individuals on that team) must also have the desire to change certain behaviors they have or develop new skills. You will find it extremely difficult to coach a team (and the individuals on that team) to achieve something they don't really want to achieve.

Ownership of the goal on the part of those being coached is critical to the coaching process. Unless you can get your team to take ownership of your business goals, you are setting yourself up for failure as a coach.

Ownership Only Comes From Self Awareness

A few years ago, I was making a presentation at a coaching conference in London. At the end of my talk, I was about to make the usual dash to the airport when I noticed Tim Gallwey (author of the **Inner Game of Tennis**) was speaking later that day. I made the decision to change my flight and stay and hear him.

At first, I was disappointed in my decision to stay as much of the early part of the presentation was Tim playing a black & white video that was over 30 years old. The tape showed Tim attempting to teach a rather hefty woman in a muumuu how to play tennis. The woman maintained that she had never been on a tennis court. That part was easy to believe as you watched her first attempts to hit the ball. Laughter started to break out in the audience.

Tim then provided a suggestion… "When the ball hits the court, say, 'Bounce!' and when your racket strikes the ball, say, 'Hit!'" As she implemented the "Bounce/Hit" technique, slowly but surely, she was able to return several forehand shots. Next, she could keep her backhand shots in play. Tim explained that the Bounce/Hit concept created self-awareness that connected the mind to what the body was doing. He continued to give the woman other suggestions for creating self-awareness as she continued to practice. Finally, she could serve.

*A coach helps you get from where you are
to where you want to be.*

Here is the unbelievable part – she was able to do all of this playing in her muumuu, using a racket she had never held in her hand before, in about 20 minutes time!

Needless to say, I was intrigued. Later that night, I had dinner with Tim Gallwey to learn more about Tim's thesis – "It is only through self-awareness that people take ownership for what they do and what happens to them."

Keep Your Eye On The Ball

Dinner that night started with a discussion about self-awareness and its role in generating ownership of our behaviors and how those behaviors affect others and us.

Tim began, "How often have you heard the phrase, 'Keep your eye on the ball?'" According to Tim, the phrase "Keep your eye on the ball!" is the most often used but least effective phrase in ball sports. As I reflected on my own days as a baseball, softball and tennis player (and current sports spectator), I had to agree. "Keep your eye on the ball!" was used far more than any other coaching directive. This is especially true of parents when they yell encouragement to their kids at little league games.

Tim continued, "Keeping your eye on the ball is the single most valuable focus in tennis and other ball sports, but the command 'Keep your eye on the ball!' won't cause you to keep your eye on the ball in a way that is meaningful and effective."

Tim, who spent his early career as a tennis coach said, "The way you get people to focus on the ball is to ask them questions."

1. "If I ask, 'Which way is the ball spinning as it comes toward you?' you can't give me an answer unless you are focused on the ball."

2. "If I ask, 'How high the ball is passing over the net after it leaves your racket?' you can't tell me without being focused on the ball."

3. "If I ask, 'How close is the ball to the baseline when you hit it?' you won't know unless you are focused on the ball."

What A Coach Really Does

Tim explained further, "If you are to respond to any of these questions, you cannot avoid watching the ball. The questions compel you to keep your eye on the ball in ways that the command, 'Keep your eye on the ball!' cannot. These questions and their answers cause you to focus at a much higher level than you normally would. That higher level of focus and attention regarding the speed, spin and trajectory of the ball feeds into your brain in a way that enables both your mind and body to process and respond with a series of almost automatic adjustments that causes you to improve your game."

Tim Gallwey's system is based on illustrating to his students that through increasing their attention, focus and perception, their brain and subsequently their body will self adjust in ways that will improve their game. The real secret to improving one's game is "within" us, not "external" to us. Tim's system regarding what goes on inside the performer is spelled out in detail in his book, **The Inner Game of Tennis** (followed by **The Inner Game of Skiing, The Inner Game of Golf**, and at the time of our dinner in London, Tim was working on a manuscript for **The Inner Game of Work**, which was published in 2000).

The Importance Of Self-Awareness In Business

Awareness takes place in one of two ways – *self-awareness* or *confrontational awareness*. Many times in the coaching process, we start with confrontational awareness (i.e., getting less than positive feedback from a recent 360° or having an individual or team badly miss their target). Your job as a coach is to help move your team from confrontational awareness to self-awareness.

Your job as coach is to move from confrontational awareness to self-awareness.

An effective way to do this is by gently and almost tentatively asking the person or group you are coaching questions about how they perceive the results of their own behavior. Remember the tennis example – the command, "keep your eye on the ball" usually doesn't accomplish much. But, questions like, "Which way is the ball spinning?" or "How high is the ball when you serve it?" can be very effective in causing us to become aware of how we impact the ball and play the game.

So it is in business. Telling your team, "Get the contract," or "Make the right decision," won't help them actually get the contract or make the right decision.

Take a moment and think of a goal that you have for your team. Make it an action statement… like "keep your eye on the ball." Write it down here.

_____

_____

_____

_____

_____

What A Coach Really Does

Now, take a moment and think of some questions that you can use with your team that will help them "keep their eye on the ball."

_____

_____

_____

_____

_____

_____

_____

_____

_____

_____

_____

_____

_____

_____

_____

_____

Asking the individuals on your team questions like these can be very effective in creating self-awareness in the players on your team (or in the entire team itself). They begin to see the link between their specific behaviors at work and results they achieve.

Coaches Know And Use The Performance Equation

One final note is in order before we close this chapter on what a coach really does. A coach, in athletics or business, understands the performance equation and how their role as a coach equates to that equation.

The Performance Equation

$$\text{Individual Performance} = \left(\left(\text{Present Ability} + \text{Potential}\right) \times \text{Correct \& Consistent Practice}\right) - \text{Noise}$$

The Performance Equation is actually a pretty simple formula. Let's take it piece by piece.

Individual Performance: Our individual performance is actually a combination of factors. Understanding or executing these factors will increase or decrease our overall level of performance. The rest of the equation determines individual performance and maximizing individual performance is the goal of every coach.

Present Ability: Our present ability is primarily the skills, knowledge and know-how we currently have at doing our job. A coach can bring an objective perspective to what our present ability actually is.

Potential: Our potential is basically our talent – the skills we can tap into and/or what we can learn to help us achieve our greatest potential. A coach can be especially helpful in recognizing and maximizing our potential.

Correct & Consistent Practice: The actions/behaviors we engage in that apply our present abilities and potential in a way that builds upon and reinforces these skills. This is another part of the equation where coaches can provide guidance and perspective.

Noise: Noise is basically all of things that distract us from being focused on our jobs and doing our jobs well. There are two types of noise: *external* and *internal*.

External noise can include the seemingly never-ending need to respond to phone calls, answer emails, go to meeting after meeting – or the guy in the next office who makes every call using his speaker phone.

Internal noise can include personal problems or concerns that occupy our minds and time during work hours. Internal noise can also include health problems or even issues of self-confidence.

To better understand the concept of noise, think about a professional basketball player at the free throw line. Behind the basket is a churning sea of literally hundreds of fans all jumping up and down, waving banners and yelling at the top of their lungs as the player prepares to take the shot. This is external noise.

As he takes his shot, the player knows that at his best, he has a 60% accuracy rating on his free throws for the season. He has already made 6 consecutive shots in this game. Can he do better than he has ever done and move to a new level of performance or will he miss the next four free throws? This is internal noise. A good coach can help people with their "noise" problems – both the internal and the external ones.

The Performance Equation

$$\text{Individual Performance} = \left(\left(\text{Present Ability} + \text{Potential}\right) \times \text{Correct \& Consistent Practice}\right) - \text{Noise}$$

All of these factors put together make up the Performance Equation. The Equation applies to individuals and can also be applied to a team as a whole.

A great coach knows that their job is to support their players in all of the elements of the equation:

- A coach helps provide an accurate assessment of present ability;

- A coach helps us recognize our highest potential;

- A coach helps us focus on correct and consistent practice, and...

- A coach helps us minimize both external and internal noise.

What A Coach Really Does

Keep the Performance Equation in mind as you move onto the next chapter where we will start outlining more specifically what it takes to coach a winning team.

Chapter 4

Coaching Your Winning Team

Ask any professional coach what the key is to a championship team and you will probably get a one-word answer – TALENT!   TALENT is also the most critical factor for winning in non-athletic organizations. So, as a coach, how do you attract talent? Many would give you another one-word answer – MONEY!

Not so fast... remember the 2001 World Series when the Arizona Diamondbacks defeated the New York Yankees (even though the total Yankee payroll was double that of the Diamondbacks).   There are lots of examples of lesser paid teams and individuals defeating their higher paid competitors.

Don't misunderstand... pay is important. You start by offering competitive pay to attract talent. But, great coaches know that in addition to competitive pay there are other factors that help attract and retain great talent.

As a coach, you want to create a winning value proposition to attract and retain great talent for your team. You want your team to be known for exciting challenges, talented and fun teammates, great performance and a caring culture.   Those qualities, in addition to competitive pay, will go a long way in helping you attract the best talent to your team. Talent is important. But remember, Carl, the center Coach Pix booted off my high-school basketball team. Talent that fits your culture is even more important.

That said... it is time to turn our attention to the realities that confront you as a coach.

Facing The Facts About Your Team

Unless your situation is far different than the work place most of us find ourselves in, not everyone on your team is a "star" player. The challenge for most of us is to lead and coach teams whose members vary greatly in terms of overall ability, specific skills and level of motivation.

Generally speaking, you can categorize the players on your team into three groups: Top Talent, Steady Performers, and Laggards. If you are fortunate, your team might look like this:

Coaching Your Winning Team

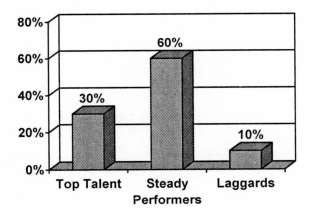

If you are not so lucky, the breakdown of your group might look more like this:

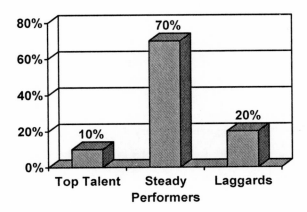

What you need to remember is that most people fall into one of these three categories and that each group on your team has special needs. Therefore, you will have to adapt your coaching to suit those different needs.

Before we address the different ways you need to coach these three groups, let's first look at some universal rules that apply to coaching all members of a winning team – no matter what type of player you are working with.

Rule 1 – Coaches Create Winning Cultures

To establish a winning culture, consider the following questions:

1. Do you really believe your team can "win?" Does your team know how you feel?

2. Is your team excited about winning? Do you keep them excited?

3. Are your expectations for both the team and individuals reasonable?

4. Are your expectations crystal clear (not just for yourself, but for your team and the individual members of your team)?

5. Do team members have the skills and training to do their work well?

6. Do you give individuals the freedom to succeed? Are there any obstacles to their performance?

7. Finally, do you embrace a culture that holds your team accountable for their performance? Do you recognize and reward good performers and do you, as a coach, provide appropriate and consistent consequences for poor performance?

How'd you do? Are you creating a winning culture for your team? If you couldn't answer with a resounding "Yes!" then you need to start.

Culture counts. Why? First, the overall culture (atmosphere) of the organization is the most important driver of employee attitude – whether employees are excited and work with passion or whether they are bored and do just enough to get by.

Second, 80% of corporate culture is determined by the leadership of the organization – leadership at every level. As coach, you determine 80% of the culture for your team – it's your choice as to whether it's a winning culture or a losing one.

Rule 2 – Coaches Practice What They Preach

For all of your players to function at their highest potential you, as coach, must practice what you preach. Consistency counts. What do we mean?

Well, don't say, "We reward performance," and then give a 3% raise across the board without taking into account individual performance. You aren't sending a consistent message to your team. Your top talent will think you don't value their contributions as much as those who don't perform as well and your laggards will think that their current level of performance is acceptable and even worth a reward.

Don't say, "Our employees are our greatest asset," and then, when the economy heads south, you decide that the first thing to be cut from the budget is employee training (or, even worse, the employees themselves). Employees know the difference between corporate "lip-service" and how their leadership really feels. It's the difference between saying and doing... so if employees are your greatest asset (which we would challenge you to deny), then treat them that way.

Don't say "We emphasize teamwork," and then implement a bonus plan that rewards individual performance only. Yes, you want to reinforce the performance of your top talent, but not to the exclusion of the rest of the team. If the "team" wins, then the "team" should be rewarded. If you realize that the wins your team has achieved have been the result of only a few top people, then you know that your team is in trouble. Not everyone is pulling their weight which means you, as coach, haven't been pulling yours.

Rule 3 – Coaches Make Sure Their Teams Know The Score

In order to win, a team has to know the score. In sports, there is always some kind of scoreboard. Players (and fans) can look up at the scoreboard at any point during the game and see the critical metrics for the game: who's winning, by how much, and how much time is left to play. Your team needs a "score board," too. One that can be easily understood by every member of the team and that measures the important metrics of what it will take to win.

Over the last few years, the corporate world has started to recognize the importance of keeping score. One popular scorekeeping device called the "balanced scorecard" was introduced. However, while many organizations now use this balanced scorecard approach, not all of them are using it successfully. To be successful with the scorekeeping approach, you must make sure that:

1) Your scorecard is measuring the right things – those things that are clearly linked to achieving the goals of the team and the organization's bottom line.

2) The items on the scorecard cannot be too numerous – too many items on the scorecard and people will get confused as to what it really takes to win the game.

3) The items on the scorecard must be constructed in a way that they are easily understood. People must be able to quickly tell when they are "winning" and when they are "losing."

4) The scorecard needs to be balanced. In addition to bottom line performance metrics, there needs to be some attention on "softer" issues of people development, sharing knowledge and know-how, and contribution to a caring team culture.

5) Finally, you may want to have a scorecard for your team and individual scorecards for each player on your team.

With the right scorecard, your team will know when they have to play defensively, offensively or when they just need to give it all they got.

Now that we have laid out the three universal rules that apply to all of your team members – let's return to those three performance groups: Top Talent, Steady Performers and Laggards.

Coaching Top Talent

Your Top Talent team members earned their top status by consistently being great performers. They do their jobs very well and sometimes take up the slack for those on your team who are not pulling their fair share. As the coach of the team, you might be tempted to think that your group of top performers don't need as much of your coaching as the rest of your team. Think again!

Coaching Your Winning Team

Top performers need your time, coaching and recognition just as much, if not more than any of your other players. You need to reinforce their top-level performance and keep them motivated. A good coach makes sure that top players feel appreciated for the great work they do.

A lack of appreciation and recognition can so demotivate a top player that their performance starts to fall off and they drop to the level of a Steady Performer… a far cry from their former glory. Or, if a player feels really under-rewarded, they might decide to go to another team where their Top Talent performance is actually recognized and appreciated.

Coaching Tips for Top Talent

1. <u>Consult with them</u>

2. <u>Delegate every time you can</u>

3. <u>Provide development opportunities</u>

4. <u>Recognition, recognition, recognition</u>

---

1. <u>Consult with them</u>: All Top Talent is motivated when someone seeks their input. If they're your best people, then they obviously know something about what it takes to win. Tap that knowledge. Ask for their input. Top Talent should frequently be involved as you map strategy, make decisions, or even when you are hiring someone. Not only will you get the benefit of their

opinions and ideas – but they'll know that you care about what they think. Letting people know that you value their opinion is one of the best motivators a coach can use.

2. <u>Delegate every time you can</u>: Your Top Talent are smart, hardworking people. They know what to do, so turn them loose. Save those micromanaging skills for the Laggards.

3. <u>Provide development opportunities</u>: Give your Top Talent training opportunities to maximize and broaden their strengths. It's one sure fire way to guarantee that your top people stay on top.

4. <u>Recognition, recognition, recognition</u>: Your Top Talent experience success more often than the others on your team. You as their coach cannot take this success for granted. Tell these top people how proud you are of them. Encourage them to celebrate when they have had success – most importantly, join them in the celebration.

Eventually, some of your top players will move on to bigger jobs with more responsibility and pay – either in your organization or somewhere else. Don't attempt to fight this or hold them back. You, as a coach, want to coach and support your Top Talent while they are on your team and continue to support them when they move on to something better. A great coach never burns bridges with Top Talent. Remember, some

Coaching Your Winning Team

day you might take on a new job of your own and be in a position to hire them back to your new team *or* they might be in a position to hire you.

Coaching Steady Performers

For many of us, this group makes up the biggest percentage of our team. Your Steady Performers are the backbone of your team. In truth, it is your effectiveness with this group that will ultimately determine your success as a coach and whether your team wins or loses.

Some of the players in this group may have previously been Top Talent and, for whatever reason, no longer perform at top levels. Others in this group may have some Top Talent behaviors but don't consistently perform in an outstanding way across the board. And, as many a sports coach can tell you, the difference between winning and losing is getting rid of inconsistent performance. Your job as coach is to determine why some of your players are inconsistent, what you can do to minimize the inconsistency, and how to motivate your players to increase their level of performance.

It should be your goal to coach all of your Steady Performers to become top talent. However, even as you are raising the bar for the Steady Performers, don't push them beyond their limits. Not everyone is "star" material. However, there have been many cases where steady and true has won the day. With your Steady Performers keeping you strongly in the game, there'll be far less need to have to scramble in the last quarter to pull a miracle play out of your hat.

So, first, recognize the value of your Steady Performers and then coach them to keep their steady progress up the performance ladder.

Coaching Tips for Steady Performers

1. Encourage a focus on the scorecard

2. Give frequent and specific feedback on performance

3. Find ways to get them interacting with Top Talent

4. Catch them performing Top Talent behavior

Coaching Tips for Steady Performers

1. Encourage a focus on the scorecard: Make sure this group sees the importance of the scorecard as an important tool to keep their performance on track as well as a basis for accountability.

2. Give frequent and specific feedback on performance: Like all groups, feedback is what drives performance for these steady contributors. Relate feedback to their current jobs but also share from time-to-time what it takes to move up to the Top Talent group.

3. <u>Find ways to get them interacting with Top Talent</u>: Your goal is to get some of this group to eventually move up to the Top Talent group. Look for ways for them to have the opportunity to work with members of the Top Talent group and pick up some of their skills and behaviors.

4. <u>Catch them performing Top Talent behavior</u>: Remember the people in this group perform Top Talent behaviors some of the time – just not all the time. So, when they do perform at the level of Top Talent, reinforce that behavior with positive feedback. Remember, behavior that gets praised and reinforced is more likely to be repeated.

Coaching Laggards

Hopefully, Laggards will make up only a small part of your team. Despite their small number, you may find yourself spending a good deal of time dealing with them.

There are many reasons why Laggards don't perform well. Remember the Performance Equation. There are several factors that can impact individual performance. Some Laggards feel they can "do just enough to get by" and still collect a paycheck. Sometimes poor performance may be due to serious personal issues, bad habits (like being chronically late), or in some cases, substance abuse.

For whatever reason, Laggards don't pull their weight on the team and, as a coach, you end up spending much of your time worrying about them. More importantly, the rest of the team rates your effectiveness as a coach by how you deal with Laggards. If you as team coach let Laggards slide on their performance without repercussions, you may see the performance of your Steady Performers, and even your Top Talent, drop.

Why?

Because people who work hard become demotivated when they see others who don't do as much receiving the same pay/benefits/rewards they do. It's the old, "Why should I put all this extra energy into winning when Bob can just slack off."

So beware! While Laggards are the toughest group for many coaches to deal with, you need to deal with them well or lose some of your effectiveness with the rest of your team.

An additional challenge in dealing with Laggards is that coaches many times have difficulty understanding the problem. If you have worked your way to a leadership position, then you most likely did so by being Top Talent yourself. If that is the case, you have very high standards for performance and it is difficult for you to understand why people don't always strive to perform at their best. So, Laggards present a particularly sticky challenge because, as a coach, you don't understand them, and thus, have a hard time coaching them.

Coaching Your Winning Team

Here, then, are some tips for coaching Laggards.

Coaching Tips for Laggards

1. Identify exactly what it is that's causing the problem

2. Get Laggards to develop their own performance improvement plan

3. Make sure they know the consequences if the plan succeeds – or if it fails

4. Enforce the consequences

Coaching Tips for Laggards

1. Identify exactly what it is that's causing the problem: You need to be specific in determining exactly why a player is considered a Laggard. Remember the Performance Equation? There are many factors that can impact individual performance. As a coach, you will want to make sure you identify exactly why your Laggard player is not performing up to standard so that you can effectively coach the individual to improve.

2. <u>Get Laggards to develop their own performance improvement plan</u>: You want to make sure that they "own" the problem and its solution. The best way to make the Laggards feel ownership is to have them take first cut at coming up with a plan for the solution. After they do – then you can make changes or recommendations. Just make sure you keep the monkey on their back – not yours.

3. <u>Make sure they know the consequence if the plan succeeds – or if it fails</u>: The Laggards are sometimes Laggards because no one has ever provided any "consequences" for being a Laggard. Your goal as coach is to structure the consequences in such a way that the Laggard will either join the ranks of the Steady Performers or they will be off the team and you can bring in a new and better player.

4. <u>Enforce the consequences</u>: Hopefully, in most cases, your coaching of the Laggards will move them into the ranks of steady performers. But, remember our definition for "to be coached." It means to carry a person from where they are to where they want to be. It is the individual, even the Laggard, who must be open to coaching. On those occasions, when you encounter someone who is not willing to be coached – it is their problem – not yours as coach. If a Laggard does not meet the goals

of the plan that you both agreed to – you have no choice. You encourage them to leave "voluntarily" or you exit them from the organization. Be fair, be even-handed and by all means consult with H.R. Documentation are especially important when you exit a non-performer. But exit non-performers you must.

As a coach, your team judges you
by how you coach the Laggards on your team.

As coach of the team, your team members evaluate you in terms of how you coach Top Talent, how you coach Steady Performers, *and* especially how you coach Laggards. You as a coach may make your greatest contribution as coach by your work with the Laggards either by coaching them to join the ranks of Steady Performers or "exiting" them from the team to open up a slot for a new member. As someone put it, 'Groom' them or 'Broom' them."

The Leader As Coach

Chapter 5

Coaching and Relational Intelligence (RQ)

You've heard of IQ (how smart you are). You may have even heard of EQ (your emotional/social intelligence). But, have you heard of RQ (relational intelligence)? It is our belief that it is a person's RQ – more than any other factor – which differentiates an average leader from a truly exceptional one. Your understanding of RQ will play a major role in your effectiveness as coach of your team.

Over the years, we have worked with thousands of leaders from almost every industry, both profit and non-profit, at all levels. The majority of these leaders (especially at higher levels) are highly intelligent... but being smart has not always guaranteed their success. In a study based on a national databank of 60,000 executives, having high levels of intelligence was found to play no significant role in determining a leader's effectiveness on the job. Indeed, many highly intelligent individuals have derailed as leaders. Why?

Well, some say it is because they lack EQ (emotional intelligence). In the decade of the 1990's, much has been said and written about a leader's emotional intelligence and how emotions and intuition play a critical role in a leader's success (or failure). EQ also emphasizes a leader's ability to "connect" with those they are trying to lead or influence.

In reality, leadership (coaching) requires using both the head (IQ) and the heart (EQ). However, neither IQ nor EQ in and of themselves can guarantee your success as a coach. Make no mistake, they are both necessary. However, the value of IQ and EQ can only be truly realized when they are utilized in the framework of a person's RQ – Relational Intelligence.

A Relational Approach To Coaching

A relational approach to coaching isn't so much about the traits and competencies a "coach" needs to be successful. It is about the *relationship*, over time, between the coach and those the coach wants to influence and motivate (their employees or other leaders). It is only within the critical context of the ongoing *relationship* that you as a leader and coach can make the most of both your IQ and EQ.

To some extent, business has acknowledged the value of building and maintaining relationships, but most of these approaches focus on relationships with customers: relationship banking, relationship marketing, etc. What has received far less attention is a focus on the relationships leaders can forge with their employees and with other leaders. It is within a relational approach that truly great coaching can manifest itself.

The Key To Coaching

What is Relational Intelligence (RQ)?

Relational intelligence (RQ) is a coach's ability to accurately perceive and utilize the dynamics of day-to-day interpersonal interactions with their team and understand how these interactions impact the relationship over time.

On a micro level: A leader's IQ and EQ do not operate independently or in a vacuum. Rather, IQ and EQ combine to play within a relational context where the history of a particular relationship greatly impacts the behavior exhibited during any specific current interaction within that relationship. In other words, your relationship history with a particular individual impacts any current interactions you have with that person. In turn, your current relational interactions with an individual will impact your future interactions with that person. Thus, relational intelligence would require that you recognize that how you related to your team in the past and how you relate to them today, will determine, to a large extent, the success or failure of the interactions you have with them in the future.

On a macro level: The relational dynamics that apply to one-on-one interactions become magnified when applied in the group setting of a team or organization. A coach's interactions with individual members of a group are combined and translated into a collective relational framework that becomes applicable across all members of the group. Thus, you as a coach not only maintain individual relationships with your employees, but you also maintain a macro-level relationship with their entire team.

Conceptualizing Relational Intelligence (RQ)

Every relational interaction is actually 3-in-1. Within any one interaction, you as coach of your team must realize the dynamics of any relational interaction you engage in.

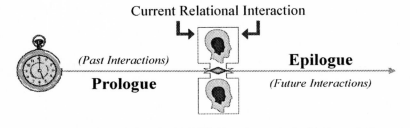

1. ***The Relational Prologue:*** the history of past interactions that have occurred in the relationship.

2. ***The Current Relational Interaction:*** the issues and dynamics at play within the context of the interaction at hand.

3. ***The Relational Epilogue:*** the impact that the current interaction, as well as all past interactions, will have on future interactions in the ongoing relationship.

The Key To Coaching

When you take a coaching approach to leadership, your most important power is influence... not command and control. As a coach, you must be aware that every interaction (both large and small) you have with your employees either adds to or detracts from the influence you have in the ongoing relationship. However, it is during the more critical interactions where relational intelligence becomes most important. It's when there is a lot at stake that you might find yourself looking back on a relationship with a member of your team and wish you had been "smarter" in how you handled the relationship in the past.

Your success as a coach depends
on how well you manage long-term relationships.

So, from the outset, you as coach need to handle <u>every</u> interaction with your employees in terms of a long-term win/win scenario. One of the keys to relational intelligence is knowing that there are times when you, as coach of your team, will want to leave something on the "relationship table" to maintain the vitality of the long-term ongoing relationship (i.e., you may need to compromise or give in a little on a less important issue so that when a big issue comes up, you've got some equity built up in the relationship).

Given the hectic pace of day-to-day, on-the-job interactions, leaders (even those who take a coaching approach) don't always take the time to think about RQ and what long-term effects their interactions might have on their team or individuals on the team. What to do?

Relational Intelligence (RQ): Getting Started

All of us have had the experience as we drift off to sleep at night of re-living a particular relational interaction that did not go well and wonder… why? The relational framework presented above might provide some insights. Did some past issue in the relationship (relational prologue) perhaps affect the current interaction in some way that you had not considered at that moment? Was the interaction tempered in terms of a long-term win/win scenario for both parties in the ongoing relationship? These questions are what RQ is all about.

In addition, there are three other considerations that might help you as coach leverage your RQ when interacting with your team.

1.   Be Aware Of Stamp Collecting

2.   Use The Right Psychological Currency

3.   Elevate Interactions To The Level Of Agreement

Let's take each one in turn and examine how being aware of these considerations can help you elevate your RQ.

The Key To Coaching

1. Be Aware Of Stamp Collecting: On occasion, you as a coach might find yourself in a situation where another person's reaction to the current situation is far more volatile than the situation would appear to justify. These excessive reactions are frequently not an accurate reflection of the current interaction but a result of some negative perceptions based on the past history of the relationship.

Maybe you're familiar with the trading stamps shoppers used to collect as a bonus for shopping in supermarkets and department stores. People pasted these stamps into little books, and when the books were filled, they could redeem them for toasters, clocks, even vacations. In relationships, we "collect" and "redeem" stamps as well, but usually the results aren't nearly as pleasant or productive.

An executive once told us about her "stamp" collection on a boss she once had early in her career. During the five years she worked for him, he did a lot of things to help her complete her stamp book. When they went out for lunch, he'd frequently be in the restroom when the check arrived. He would tell visitors to park in her parking place. He frequently took credit for her ideas and work. He made condescending remarks about women and insulted his own boss behind the boss' back. All during that time, the woman was mentally collecting her stamps of her boss' relational interactions with her.

Then, it was time to cash in the stamp book. A question arose about an expense report her boss had put in for payment. There was a mistake on the report claiming he had made a trip he had never taken. Now, her boss had always filled out and put in his own expense reports. However, when someone from accounting stopped in to check on it, her boss, in front of her, claimed she had made an error. The woman quit on the spot.

Her boss probably had no idea how many stamps he had accumulated in her relational stamp book. He probably thought she would just accept the blame without question. However, because of his considerable lack of RQ, he was completely unprepared when a "relatively" minor interaction resulted in her having collected the final stamp in her "relational stamp book" and triggered such a strong response from his employee.

2. Use The Right Psychological Currency: With every interaction you have, you as a coach should work to build win/win relationships with your employees. However, you must take care that what you contribute to the relationship is actually something the other person values.

How much is one dollar worth? A dollar will probably buy you the same cup of coffee in California as it will in Florida. The exchange rate is the same on the East and West Coasts. When you travel to a foreign country, the exchange rate is usually fixed as well. One dollar will get you approximately 10 pesos, 2 marks, 7 francs, 120 yen, and so on, depending on the exchange rate that day. In our economic transactions, the currencies are tangible and the rate of exchange is fixed.

The Key To Coaching

In our relational interactions, we exchange "currencies" as well. But most of these relational currencies are not tangible and the exchange rate is rarely fixed.

In many instances, leaders have gone to great lengths to give something to the relationship that the other person doesn't really value (i.e., they offer them the wrong psychological currency). In order to know what is actually valued and desired by the other individual in the relationship, you as a coach must be able to engage in clear and open communication. Sometimes, this will involve putting aside personal agendas and issues so that you can really listen to what the other individual is trying to communicate. However, take care to not only listen to the words being spoken, but also listen between the lines. In reality, only 7% of communication is language. The other 93% of communication is expressed non-verbally. So, coach, use your RQ – be sure to listen to the *total* message being communicated, make sure you know what it is your employees want/need from their relationship with you and that they really know what you want/need from them.

3. Elevate Interactions To The Level Of Agreement: When one of our relational interactions turns into a disagreement, the standard reaction is for both parties in the interaction to become defensive and delve into great detail in order to support their individual positions. As a coach, the more relationally intelligent approach to dealing with disagreement would be to elevate the interaction back up to a level where everyone is in agreement. Then, from a point of agreement, the interaction can continue on to more specific issues.

For example, how many times have you been in a meeting where three different departments or divisions of your business were represented and they all had their own agendas and wanted different things. Most likely, the meeting quickly spiraled down into chaos where everyone closed themselves off to the group and only focused on what "they" wanted.

The next time this happens, you, as a relationally "smart coach," should stop the downward spiral and get everyone clear on the fact that, though they may represent different departments or divisions, they are still on the same team – and they are all trying to win the game. From that perspective, the meeting could progress from a level of agreement with all parties focused on the same macro level goal. If the discussion began to spiral down again, it's up to you to go back up to the level of mutual agreement whenever you reach an apparent impasse with your team or a member of your team.

High RQ = Win/Win Relationships

Leadership (coaching) really is a combination of IQ (the head) and EQ (the heart). But both IQ and EQ only reach their greatest potential when they are employed within a relational RQ framework.

The Key To Coaching

Relational intelligence requires that instead of trying to get the most benefit out of every single interaction, that as a coach, you will want to focus on the long-term benefits of your ongoing relationship... even if that means sacrificing an immediate benefit in order to maximize the relationship over the long-term. Exceptional coaches use their relational intelligence to make the most of all relationships, even ones where mutual benefit can only be found in ending the relationship. However, the primary focus for coaches with high levels of RQ is to build and maintain long-term win/win relationships.

The Leader As Coach

Chapter 6

The Key to Coaching –

Feedback, Feedback, Feedback

Feedback regarding performance is what taps into that competitive transistor that is inside all of us. The world of spectator sport is flooded with feedback. Of course, there is a scoreboard that lets us know who's winning, who's losing and how much time is left to play. There is feedback from your teammates, and at the end of the game, sometimes feedback from the competition. Finally, there is feedback from the coach. That's the deal with sports.

In the world of business, it is usually quite a different story. As coach of your business team, most of the burden for providing feedback falls squarely on your shoulders and it is crucial that you understand the connection between feedback and performance. This really is the most important chapter of this book in terms of your effectiveness as coach.

Let's start with a story.

It was his first circus. His grandfather had promised to take him on his next birthday, and now they were there. The smells of cotton candy and peanuts tickled his nose. He was mystified by the astonishing feats the circus animals performed. He watched wide-eyed as the elephants knelt down and rolled over like his dog, then stood majestically on their hind legs. His head bobbed as the horses trotted in line around the center ring, while riders jumped on and off the horses' backs at will. But his mouth popped open and his eyes bulged as a huge male lion leaped fluidly about a caged ring, climbed a ladder, crept along a narrow board suspended nearly 15 feet in the air, then jumped through a large, flaming hoop.

He tugged on his grandfather's sleeve and whispered excitedly, "Grandpa, grandpa, how do they get the lion to do that?"

"Do what, son?"

"How do they get the lion to jump through the hoop when it's on fire?"

The old man looked down and smiled at his grandson. "Well, it's like this. They go out in the jungle, set a hoop on fire, hang it from a tree, and wait. They capture the first lion which jumps through the hoop and bring it back to the circus."

The boy's brow knotted. "Is that really how they do it, grandpa?"

Feedback, Feedback, Feedback

"No, not really. They actually go out into the jungle and look for a lion, preferably a young one. Then they catch him, bring him back to the circus, and train him," the grandfather said,

Then the grandfather, who knew something about these matters, explained the whole process. Now, when the lion first begins training, a hoop which is not on fire is placed on ground level in a ring. The lion walks around the ring, and eventually walks through the hoop. As soon as he does, the trainer gives him some meat. When he walks through the hoop again, the trainer gives the lion more meat. Pretty soon, the lion figures out that going through the hoop means lunch.

As the grandson listened intently, and the "ooohs" and "aaaahs" of the crowd surrounded them, the grandfather explained that, bit by bit, the trainer raises the hoop, and the lion learns he has to jump through it in order to get more meat. Soon the hoop is 15 feet high. Most lions can't jump that high, so they have to climb a ladder and edge along a catwalk so they can get to the hoop.

The grandfather paused to sneeze. After he put his handkerchief back in his pocket, he explained that it was at this point that the trainer set the hoop on fire.

"Fire scares lions, of course," he said, glancing out at the center ring, where a lion was jumping through another flaming hoop. "But they crave fresh meat even more. So the lion learns that jumping through the flaming hoop earns him a lot more meat, and he's willing to do it. It's a lot easier than going hunting in the jungle."

The boy paused, looked out at the center ring, then turned to his grandfather. "But, Grandpa. Why does the lion tamer keep cracking the whip like that?"

The old man chuckled. "That's just for show, my boy. The lion could care less and his master knows it."

You're probably not in the business of taming lions – though you may sometimes feel like it when you're trying to coach your team on the job. But this story has two important morals:

- People (like lions) perform better when they get feedback on their performance.

- People perform better when the feedback they get is positive.

Think again about the things you like to do when you're off the job. One reason you like these activities is that they give you something to shoot for. Most of them also give you feedback about your performance. You see what happens when you hit a

Feedback, Feedback, Feedback

golf ball, serve a tennis ball, watch your garden grow, land a striped bass or hear the sound of your favorite musical instrument when you play it.

At work, though, we often don't get feedback. Instead, we have to wait until someone tells us how we're doing. Too often, we think the wait will last forever – unless the feedback is negative. Then we hear about it right away.

In many organizations, we lead by exception:

> *If you don't hear from me, that means*
> *you're doing OK. But make a mistake,*
> *and I'll climb down your throat.*

Using this kind of management, many leaders do crack the whip... and it's not just for show. When, for example, was the last time you called a meeting to give someone a pat on the back for doing something right? When was the last time you sat down with your team to list all the things that they do well?

Negative feedback, a verbal kick in the rump, is simply a form of punishment. When people get negative feedback, they often want to give less, not more, to you and to the organization.

That's not good.

Sometimes, though, you've got to give negative feedback. Later in the chapter, we'll show you how to do it productively.

In the meantime, though, if you emphasize positive feedback, letting people know how well they are doing, you'll be surprised at how rarely you need to use negative feedback when managing work relationships. But you've got to give positive feedback well, or it won't work.

Qualities of Effective Positive Feedback

If you believe in the power of positive feedback, then you'll probably recognize the four qualities that make positive feedback work. Feedback should be:

1. Immediate

2. Specific

3. Tied to performance

4. Genuine

Let's take a look at each of these qualities in more detail.

1. Feedback Should Always Be Immediate: When you whack a golf ball on the golf course, you know almost instantly how far down the fairway (or into the woods) it's going to travel. In tennis, the ball is either in or out. And when you bowl, you actually get to see the pins fall.

Feedback, Feedback, Feedback

Unfortunately, the only feedback many people get is at performance review time. That could be once every three months, six months, a year or even longer. One company actually schedules these ego-threatening events on the employee's birthday!

In most jobs, people don't get the kind of immediate feedback they do when playing golf or tennis. That's where you come in. As the coach, an important part of your job is to give frequent feedback, especially when employees are doing something that doesn't in itself give immediate feedback. Feedback is so essential that it's at the core of numerous management-training programs for business leaders at every level within organizations. Still, we can't help but wonder whether all of this training actually helps.

The Feedback Gap

Nearly 15 years ago we developed a survey to see how well leaders and their subordinates were communicating. Consider the following statement managers find on the survey:

> ### *I Let My Subordinates Know When They Are Doing A Good Job*

Managers chose an option that shows how often they actually do this. Here are their choices. Pick one for yourself:

Always	Frequently	Occasionally	Seldom	Never
☐	☐	☐	☐	☐

If you picked Always or Frequently, then you responded the same way more than 3,000 other leaders throughout the country answered. In fact, on a scale of 1 (never) to 5 (always), the average response for leaders is 4.3. Judging from their own point of view, leaders are doing a pretty terrific job of giving their subordinates feedback for work well done.

Hold on.

We then presented the following statement to a representative sample of the subordinates for those 3,000 leaders:

My Supervisor Lets Me Know When I'm Doing A Good Job

We also asked them to pick one of the following five options as to just how often their supervisor gave them positive feedback. Pick the one that pegs how often your own supervisor tells you that you're doing a good job:

Always	Frequently	Occasionally	Seldom	Never
☐	☐	☐	☐	☐

The Feedback Gap

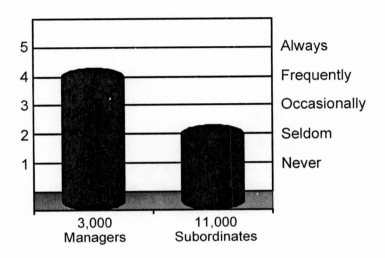

The Feedback Gap: A 200% difference between the amount of positive feedback managers say they give and the amount of positive feedback subordinates say they get.

Ooops. If you're like the nearly 11,000 people at all levels of the organization who have responded to our survey, you didn't choose Always, or even Frequently. On the same 1 to 5 scale, the average score is only 2.3! We have dubbed this canyon-sized chasm – where leaders give themselves 4.3 for giving feedback and their subordinates score them at a measly 2.3 – **The Feedback Gap**. That's a nearly 200% difference between what leaders think they provide in terms of positive feedback and what subordinates actually register. And, as coach, remember, their perception is their reality!

The facts would probably say that the truth is somewhere between 2.3 and 4.3. But the only perception that counts is the one which produced the 2.3 score. When employees say they don't get much feedback, whether true or not, it's a perception in need of repair. In your relationships with the people who work for you, you need to face this fact: They probably think you don't give nearly as many pats on the back as you think you do. And, you can't afford to wait until these people quit or get promoted to ask, "Did I give you enough feedback?" No, you've got to address this situation squarely and immediately. If you want to manage relationships effectively, then catch your people in the act of doing something right. Then tell them so. Right away.

2. Feedback Should Be Specific: Specific feedback tells people exactly how they did. In many of our recreational activities, it's really easy to know how we did. Bowlers can see how many pins were knocked down; golfers can see how

Feedback, Feedback, Feedback

close the ball is to the cup. Relationships are a lot more vaporous. When people do give pats on the back, they're usually wrapped in generalities like, "You're doing a great job," or "Thanks for the good work."

That's not to say that, as coach, you shouldn't pay general compliments to people. But specific statements have a higher payoff than general statements do. They also buttress peoples continuing to do what you want them to do in the way you want them to do it. Tell people that the way they did a specific job was terrific and they're likely to do it that way again. Suppose, instead of saying, "Great job," you said any (maybe even all) of the following:

- "Thanks for getting this report done so fast."

- "I'm really impressed by the way you were able to pull the information together so quickly."

- "It's great to have someone I can count on to keep a cool head when we have tough situations."

People, including you, want recognition for their unique contribution to relationships. They want to stand out. Specific feedback lets people know that you recognize how special their contributions actually are and that you have noticed and prize the talents and qualities they bring to their relationship with you and the team.

3. Feedback Should Be Tied To Performance: Effective feedback is not just immediate and specific. It also is tied directly to performance. Some years ago a consulting firm marketed a wristwatch with nine stems, a real one and eight dummies. The dummy stems were colored red, and all anyone could do with them was to pull them out or push them in.

The idea was for "leaders" to wear this watch in the morning with all eight dummy stems out. Then, between 8 a.m. and 9 a.m., the leader would approach one of his or her subordinates and say, "You're doing great work for us. We really appreciate it." Then the leader would walk away, punching in one of the dummy stems. The ritual would be repeated each hour. By day's end, the leader would have given eight pats on the back, timed by the red reminders on the leader's wrist.

The watch was helpful because it reminded leaders to give feedback to their subordinates. Maybe this approach seems corny or silly, but many leaders who get caught up in other matters during a day desperately need reminding to give their employees feedback on their performance. However, this watch device had a major flaw. The pats on the back were tied to time – one per hour – not to a subordinate's actual performance.

Just going around giving people a cookie-cutter thank you doesn't work. If positive feedback isn't pegged to something specific the employee has done, then it is nearly worthless for the employee. The employee may even see it as an empty, even manipulative gesture, rather than a sincere attempt to give praise.

Of course, the other problem with the wristwatch approach is that it didn't take into account whether the employees actually were doing a good job. The wristwatch only encouraged leaders to give praise often, not just when it was deserved. The critical issue here is that as a leader and coach, you have to give the people who report to you feedback that is immediate, specific *and* pegged to real performance. Which boils down to this – for feedback to be effective, it has to be genuine.

4. Feedback Should Be Genuine: Some people have told us they don't like the wristwatch approach because it's too gimmicky. They're probably right. Lots of gimmicks work, but probably not this one. It prompts leaders to dish out praise, not because it's deserved, but simply because it's time to do it again. Employees aren't stupid. They can tell when you're faking it. If they think your praise is insincere, they won't think much of your pat on the back, or of you, for giving it.

Look. You want people to be genuine with you. You have to return the favor. For many leaders, though, giving praise feels awkward, and your awkwardness can come off as being insincere, even if you're not. The solution for you in your role as coach is simple. Practice, practice, practice.

If you want to be a coach who gives genuine feedback, then do exactly that. Over and over. After a while, doing it will become a natural part of your relationship with the people who report to you, and probably others as well. If you give pats on the back routinely and tie them to performance, your employees won't have any doubt about how genuine they are. If you make giving sincere praise as much a part of your day as putting on your shoes in the morning, then people will see it as a natural part of what you bring with you to work. Any possible mistrust of your sincerity will evaporate.

To recap, positive feedback works for you as a coach when you:

1. Give it right away

2. Make it specific

3. Tie it to performance

4. Make it genuine

This kind of four-fold feedback is extremely potent because it gives employees loads of payoffs they want from their work. With those payoffs comes an increased sense of getting a lot for giving a lot. People get an increased sense of equity. And with more equity, you'll find people do better work.

Feedback, Feedback, Feedback

A Special Kind of Positive Feedback - NRBs

Many organizations give rewards, perhaps a five-year gold pin, then an emerald-and-gold pin for a 10-year employee. If someone works for the company 20 years, then maybe diamonds will find their way into that pin. These rewards, however, are based on a single factor – survival. The message is:

> *Survive the job, your boss and the company,*
> *and you'll get another reward.*

These time-honored traditions have their uses, but too many companies are inhabited by people who are merely survivors, not winners. That's a shame. Too many people never get a taste of what it's like to be a winner. The power of novel rewarding behaviors – those things we do for employees that are both pleasant and unexpected – is to celebrate winners rather than those who merely survive.

Some years ago, an executive we know was appointed to the presidency of a large commercial construction company. When he took control, the company was nearly bankrupt. One of his first acts was to sign a contract with a large corporation for his company to build an office building in 13 months at a cost of $23 million. When he signed that contract, he knew he couldn't do the job within 13 months. Nor would $23 million begin to cover his company's costs. But he needed the business, so he took his chances.

But he also did a lot more. Late one evening, he visited the construction site to check on the building's progress. The foundation was being laid, and he noticed something striking. Some workers had laid cement blocks, the main components of the foundation, nearly eight feet high. Other workers across the construction site had built their blocks only three or four feet high. Obviously, some people were performing well, and others were barely crawling along, doing marginal or, at best, average work.

The president walked to his car and took out some envelopes and paper. Then he walked back to the construction site. As he passed the areas where people had met or exceeded his performance expectations, he stopped and wrote a note that simply said, "Thanks for doing a great job." Then he took a twenty-dollar bill from his wallet, wrapped it inside the note, put the note and the money in the envelope, and left it there. That night he spent almost $400 of his own money. But it was worth it. As he later told us, "You should have seen people laying cement blocks the next day."

This event wasn't a one-time quirk. The president rewarded both quality and quantity of performance on that building in other unexpected ways: catered lunches, T-shirts, decals for hard hats, more cash bonuses, and even on-the-spot pay raises for exceptional work. In total, he spent $48,000 on novel rewarding behaviors while the building was being constructed. But his people finished the building two months early and for almost $100,000 under the contract price.

Feedback, Feedback, Feedback

Today, this executive is still president of the company. He also owns it. And when he negotiates contracts for office buildings, he insists that the contract price include money to pay for his novel rewarding behaviors program. In return, he can assure buyers that they're getting a quality building which will be completed on time and on budget. He's a great coach -- a genuine winner, but his employees are, too. Being showered with novel rewarding behaviors (NRBs for short), means that he's showing his people that he recognizes and appreciates their high-quality performance.

NRB's, used effectively, can be a potent tool
for motivating your team.

NRBs at Work

Unlike our construction executive friend, you don't have to spend thousands of dollars to begin an NRB program. Of course, $48,000 was pocket change compared to what he got in return. But here's a list of NRBs which don't cost much but that enrich your relationship with your people and can help make spontaneous winners out of survivors:

- Afternoons or days off

- Personal thank-you notes

- Achievement decals for hard hats, badges for uniforms and T-shirts

- Tickets to sporting or cultural events

- Gift certificates to restaurants or day spas

This list is barely a beginning of possible NRBs you could use. Most likely, you can think of even more and better ways to reward your employees.

A Word of Caution

At work, NRBs can help boost the egos of everyday survivors and make them feel like winners. But there are some yellow caution flags to consider as you ponder ways to use NRBs:

- Be sure you're using the right currency for your employees. Not everyone will appreciate a T-shirt, or a ticket to a ball game.

- Don't forget that NRBs should be spontaneous. If you take employees to lunch two birthdays in a row, the novelty will wear off. What's worse, they might come to think of the birthday lunch as part of their benefits package.

Feedback, Feedback, Feedback

- NRBs, just like positive feedback, should be tied directly to the performance of the team or an individual employee.

Developmental
The Dilemma of Giving ~~Negative~~ Feedback

Sometimes, though, you as coach have to give people negative feedback. Part of your role as a great coach is to keep people from doing things you don't want them to do. However, feedback doesn't have to be negative. Instead, it can be *developmental*. The difference between the two is simply the difference between being constructive and destructive. Developmental feedback makes a person aware that one of their *behaviors* is inappropriate and is designed to prevent that *behavior* from occurring again. Negative feedback, on the other hand, usually doesn't target the inappropriate behavior(s), but rather makes a person feel that they are being criticized or belittled.

Some years ago, management expert Douglas MacGregor outlined what he called the *Hot Stove Principles of Punishment*. All of us learned early in life that if we put our hand on a hot stove, our hand will get burned. The resulting pain of this action is severe enough to remind us never to intentionally do it again. From this analogy, MacGregor developed several principles that can be translated and applied to other forms of "punishment."

We've adapted MacGregor's principles here to give you, in your role as coach, five guidelines for giving developmental feedback to your employees to prevent them from repeating behaviors that are undesirable.

Guideline 1: If you touch a hot stove, you get burned right away. In work relationships, our reaction to undesirable behavior is not always immediate. Many leaders wait days, even weeks, to tell an employee that they're unhappy about something the employee did. Sometimes leaders put off this unpleasant communication so long that the employee doesn't have a clear idea what the punishment is for. As we have said before, effective positive feedback should be immediate. Effective developmental feedback should be, too. If you as coach need to do it, do it quickly.

Guideline 2: The hot stove punishment is intense the very first time you touch it. At work, we tend to give developmental feedback fairly gently the first time around. If it happens again, then we're likely to be a little more harsh. If it happens again, we use even stronger punishment. That's the wrong approach. If your developmental feedback is appropriately intense the first time, you probably won't have to repeat it.

Guideline 3: The hot stove punishes only the hand that touches it. When you touch the hot stove, your whole body doesn't get burned, only your hand. When giving developmental feedback to employees, we often get too

Feedback, Feedback, Feedback

personally involved, sometimes to the point of losing our temper. So, instead of focusing on the behavior, we end up punishing the entire person. The focus of developmental feedback should be on changing the specific behavior(s) a person is engaging in that are inappropriate. Remember Coach, you're not trying to squash the entire person. If you keep your objectivity and focus only on the specific behavior(s), then your feedback will have a much better chance of affecting only those behaviors, not the whole person.

Guideline 4: The hot stove is universally consistent. No matter whose hand touches the hot stove, the hand gets burned. At work, we're sometimes tempted to punish one person for acting a particular way, but to let other people doing the same thing just slide by. Don't do this. This kind of inconsistency makes people wonder what their leaders really want or whether they're playing favorites. You, as coach, can't afford to have people who work for you wondering about either situation. Your reaction should be consistent, no matter whose behavior it is that needs to be changed.

Guideline 5: If you touch a hot stove, you have ways to stop the pain. If your hand hurts when you touch the hot stove, you can move it and stop the pain. Sometimes at work, leaders punish the way someone is acting, but don't say what these people should have done instead. Bad move. For developmental feedback to work, people need to know what they **should have done** or what **they can do** to avoid the hot stove again.

If you think through these five guidelines and apply them the next time someone is behaving in a way that is inappropriate, you'll have a much better chance of snuffing out the problem before it becomes a major issue.

But, and this point can't be stressed enough, you'll be far more effective as coach when you use positive feedback frequently. Use developmental feedback only when necessary. Indeed, using positive feedback will cut down on the number of times you have to pull out your developmental feedback skills. People would much rather know when they're doing something right, but too often we simply don't tell them and just end up cooking them on the hot stove.

Chapter 7

The Coaching Scorecard

Up to now, this book has been focused on how you, as a leader, can coach your team to win. However, there is one final element that needs to be addressed. How do you know you are being effective as a coach? How do you know your actions and behaviors are in line with being a good coach?

Or... if you are in a position where you are receiving coaching, either by your immediate leader or an outside source, how can you tell if *they* are doing a good job as *your* coach?

The answer is, you need a scorecard. You need a way to be able to measure what it takes to be an effective coach. And this scorecard needs to measure the right things. In baseball, you can be the player with the most number of hits and still lose the game. So, as a coach (or a person being coached), you need to know the right things to measure in order to gauge the effectiveness of a coaching effort.

There is a combination of factors at work for you to be a good coach (or know that you are working with one). Let's see what they are.

Scorecard Dimensions

Dimension 1: Feedback ➔ Self-Awareness ➔ Self-Motivation

The first dimension in determining the effectiveness of a coach is to gauge whether a coach has supplied ample *feedback* to the person being coaching in such a way as to bring about *self-awareness*.

If you remember back to Chapter 3, we talked about the difference between confrontational awareness and self-awareness. To be an effective coach, you have to deliver feedback in such a way that it moves a person from confrontational awareness (i.e., the coach *tells* the person they need to develop in certain areas) to self-awareness (i.e., the person being coached internally acknowledges their development needs). Why? It is self-awareness that is the basis for *self-motivation*. What does this mean? Well, let's use an example.

It is said that over 66% of the U.S. population is overweight. If you were a coach working with an overweight individual, you could share this bit of information with that person but what would their reaction be?

"You're right! A large percentage of the population is overweight. I see them every time I go out to eat."

The Coaching Scorecard

So, let's take it a step further. You take your overweight individual and put them on a scale, measure their body fat ratio, test their aerobic fitness, etc. You then compile all of this information into a pretty report. You show them on paper that they are 50 pounds overweight, have over 26% body fat and could probably not make it up two flights of stairs without collapsing. Again, what could their reaction be?

"Oh, I thought I weighed more than that! If I have 26% body fat then that must mean that I'm 74% muscle. And, I can always just use the elevator."

Okay, Coach! You've got a challenge here. So, you go to the next level. You have to somehow convince them that they need to change – not for your sake, but for their own. You tell your overweight individual...

"Look, here's what the data says... you're quite a bit overweight, you're out of shape and you really need to tone up. You have told me that one of the things you cherish most in life is being able to watch your kids grow up. Well, realistically, if you keep on the same course you are on now (overeating, no exercise), you are putting your health in jeopardy. There is a strong likelihood that as your kids get older, you could develop some serious health problems due to your weight issue – some of which could potentially be life-threatening."

"What you need to understand is that your current frame of mind and conditioning is imperiling your long-term personal goal to stay healthy enough to watch your kids grow into adults and have children of their own."

Now, what do you think their reaction is going to be?

"Wow! I never looked at it that way... [self-awareness]. From that perspective, I really see that I need to do something to change from where I currently am to where I want to be in the future... [self-motivation]."

As a coach, part of your effectiveness comes from elevating feedback from simple numbers or comments to something that will increase a person's self-awareness to the point that they are motivated within themselves to change.

Dimension 2: Tools, Techniques, Training

The second dimension in determining the effectiveness of a coach is whether or not they are able to provide specific *tools*, *techniques* and *training* suited to the individual that will help them achieve their goals. There are a multitude of tools, techniques and training you can use. To list them here is beyond the scope of this book. But, as you research and learn about different tools, techniques and training available for you to use – and before you recommend them to the person you are coaching – you will want to be sure they are specific, targeted, and build upon one another.

The Coaching Scorecard

Going back to your newly self-aware and self-motivated overweight coachee, you cannot simply tell them, "Go out and exercise." As their coach, you have to supply them with the appropriate means for them to work through their transformation. This means supply them with tailored and specific tools, techniques and training that are in line with the talents and skills the individual already has.

For instance, if the individual you are coaching has knee problems, you don't want to suggest that they start jogging. If the individual you are coaching is a diabetic, you don't want to recommend that they go on an all fruit diet. Instead, you select tools, techniques and training best suited for their current situation and condition.

If they say they like dancing, find them an invigorating dance class or even a Jazzercise class. If they like to be outdoors, have them try hiking, biking, roller-blading, walking, skipping… anything that they can physically do while enjoying being outdoors. If they don't have much time for exercise, get them started with a short but effective program that they feel won't impose on their already busy schedule.

Also, you want to make sure that the tools, techniques and training build on one another. For instance, you wouldn't want to have the person you are coaching attending a training seminar on advance macrobiotic cooking if they did not even have a simple understanding of basic nutrition. Similarly, you would not want them engaging in a weight lifting program if they did not have a strong understanding of correct body alignment and the difference between the effects of aerobic versus anaerobic activity on the body.

So, as a coach, your job is to provide specific and appropriate tools, techniques and training to the person you are coaching to help them best meet their goals.

Dimension 3: Support, Encouragement, Caring

The third dimension in determining the effectiveness of a coach is how well a coach *supports* and *encourages* the person they are coaching as well as whether they show the person that they truly *care* just as much about reaching that person's goals as the person does.

Inevitably when we are learning new skills and are adapting to new behavior patterns, we run into challenges. Your job as coach is to keep the person you are coaching motivated by supporting and encouraging them through these challenges.

For a person trying to lose weight, when they want to go off their diet, you support them by being there to help them keep strong. When they get tired and want to quit a tough exercise routine, you support them by helping them to keep going. If they have questions or concerns about what they are doing, you support them by finding the answers.

The Coaching Scorecard

You also need to encourage them. When the person you are coaching completes an exercise routine, you are there to tell them they did a great job. When they call you to tell you that their "tight" jeans are now loose, you provide genuine feedback and praise about their great accomplishment.

Most importantly, as an effective coach, you must show the person you are coaching that you care enough about them to help them through each step in the process. This doesn't mean that you wait for them to call and ask for your help. You are actively and wholeheartedly involved as they work to meet their goals. If you don't care... why should they? It is basic human nature that people need acknowledgement and recognition from others. We crave it. So, feed the need, Coach.

Dimension 4: Appropriate Measurements and Metrics

The final dimension of a good coach is how well you quantify and measure their progress. This is where you give *them* a scorecard, Coach. You keep the person you are coaching motivated by giving them targets to shoot for and showing them that they have successfully reached those targets. And, you have got to make sure you are measuring the right thing.

It is critical that the targets and goals you set for the person you are coaching are specific. You can tell them that they should stick to a 2,000-calorie a day diet... but if all those calories come from hot fudge sundaes or French fries, the measure of their calories isn't in line with their goals of a healthful lifestyle. Just measuring caloric intake isn't going to help them reach the level of health and fitness that they want.

Also, you must make the targets and goals realistic. If you set a goal that the individual runs 3 miles a day for the next six weeks and they fail week after week to achieve this goal, they will become frustrated and give up on their goal *and* on you as their coach. Set realistic, doable goals. You have to give people the feeling they are winning; all of us are more likely to stick to a plan that gives us lots of chances to achieve small victories.

Another aspect is that you need to be sure that the targets and metrics you set actually lead to the final goal. Would reading 10 books about dieting and exercise necessarily lead to weight loss? Would watching an exercise video alone get a body into shape? If you are measuring how many books your client has read or how many videos they've watched, you will show them as being successful... yet they will never reach their goal. You have to make sure you are applying the appropriate metrics. You have to measure the right things.

Finally, a coach knows to make their measurement metrics frequent enough to allow for modifications and adjustments to the plan. You don't want discover six months down the road that what the person you are coaching is doing is not getting the results they want. Check the metrics frequently. If the metrics are not moving the person toward their goal, re-evaluate the metrics to see if a change in metrics is in order.

So, in summary, as a good coach, you need to measure the progress of the person you are coaching. You and they must measure specific and realistic things. You and they must measure the right things. And, you must measure often enough to keep things on track.

Scorecard Synergy

For those of you paying attention, you will notice that the Scorecard Dimensions are put together in such a way that they give a general outline for how a coaching effort would be structured. You would start with **Feedback** ➔ **Self-Awareness** ➔ **Self-Motivation**; then flow to **Tools, Techniques, Training**; then on to **Support, Encouragement and Caring**; and finally to **Appropriate Measures and Metrics**.

You may have also observed that the final dimension of **Appropriate Measures and Metrics** leads right back into **Feedback** ➔ **Self-Awareness** ➔ **Self-Motivation**, continuing the cycle.

Now, while this basic structure is a good way to start a coaching initiative, you will find that you may need to address different dimensions at different times, not always holding to the pattern. However, the Scorecard Dimensions can act as a guide to how you can initially sequence your actions as a coach.

Scoring the Scorecard

Below are two scorecards I have developed to determine if a coaching effort is effective. The first on is for you if you *are* the coach. The second is for you if you are the person *being* coached.

Am I A Good Coach?

THE COACHING SCORECARD

AM I A GOOD COACH?

Dimension 1: Feedback → Self-Awareness → Self-Motivation

Based on a scale of 1 to 10, I provide feedback in such a way to raise the level of self-awareness in the person(s) I am coaching and, in turn, increase their self-motivation to change.

1	2	3	4	5	6	7	8	9	10

Specifically, how have I shared feedback so that I have expanded their self-awareness and motivated them to change?

Comments:

The Coaching Scorecard

Dimension 2: Tools, Techniques, Training

Based on a scale of 1 to 10, I provide the person I am coaching with tools, techniques and training suited to their individual needs in order to help them achieve their goals.

1	2	3	4	5	6	7	8	9	10

Specifically, what tools have I offered the person I am coaching to help them reach their goals and are they suited to their needs?

Comments:

Dimension 3: Support, Encouragement, Caring

Based on a scale of 1 to 10, I provide the person I am coaching with support and encouragement as they work toward their goals and I show them that I care about the achievement of their goals.

1	2	3	4	5	6	7	8	9	10

In what ways do I show my support and encouragement to the person I am coaching as they work towards their goals? Specifically, how do I show I care about them and their progress?

Comments:

Dimension 4: Appropriate Measures and Metrics

Based on a scale of 1 to 10, I frequently measure the progress of the person I am coaching using specific, realistic, appropriate and frequent metrics.

1	2	3	4	5	6	7	8	9	10

Specifically, how do I measure their progress? Are the metrics used specific, realistic, appropriate and frequent?

Comments:

Do I Have A Good Coach?

THE COACHING SCORECARD

DO I HAVE A GOOD COACH?

Dimension 1: Feedback ➔ Self-Awareness ➔ Self-Motivation

Based on a scale of 1 to 10, my coach provides feedback in such a way to raise my self-awareness and, in turn, is increasing my self-motivation to change.

1	2	3	4	5	6	7	8	9	10

Specifically, how has he/she shared feedback so that I have expanded my self-awareness so that I am self-motivated to change?

Comments:

Dimension 2: Tools, Techniques, Training

Based on a scale of 1 to 10, my coach provides me with tools, techniques and training suited to my individual needs in order to help me achieve my goals.

1	2	3	4	5	6	7	8	9	10

Specifically, what tools has my coach offered me to help me reach my goals and are they suited to my needs?

Comments:

The Coaching Scorecard

Dimension 3: Support, Encouragement, Caring

Based on a scale of 1 to 10, my coach provides his or her support and encouragement as I work toward my goals and shows that he or she cares about the achievement of goals.

1	2	3	4	5	6	7	8	9	10

In what ways does my coach show his or her support and encouragement as I work towards my goals? Specifically, how does he or she show that they care about me and my progress?

Comments:

Dimension 4: Appropriate Measures and Metrics

Based on a scale of 1 to 10, my coach frequently measures my progress using specific, realistic, appropriate and frequent metrics.

1	2	3	4	5	6	7	8	9	10

Specifically, how does my coach measure my progress? Are the metrics used specific, realistic, appropriate and frequent?

Comments:

Based on the score you assigned yourself (or your coach), you will want to plot your effectives on the 1 to 10 scale on the following chart. To determine your effectiveness as a coach, you would want to have your score on each dimension fall into

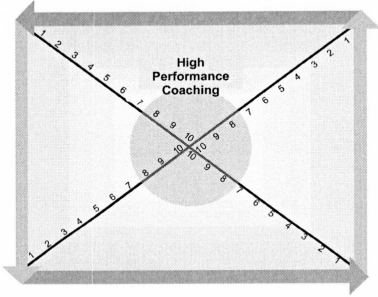

Dimension 4:
Appropriate Measures and Metrics

Dimension 3:
Support ➔ Encouragement ➔ Caring

Dimension 1:
Feedback ➔ Self-awareness ➔ Self-motivation

Dimension 2:
Tools, Techniques, Training

the middle circle. When you are in the middle circle, you know that either you, yourself, or the coach you are working with is a "High Performance Coach."

If there is a score outside of the circle and you are doing the coaching, you will want to place more emphasis on that dimension to get you to a higher level of performance.

If you are evaluating a coach you are working with and they score outside of the circle, you will want to discuss having

The Coaching Scorecard

them provide you more assistance in regard to that dimension. There is no rule that says you can't "coach" the coach.

Well, that's it, Coach. As they say – the ball is in your court.

Good luck!

The Leader As Coach

Appendix A

Coaching Your Boss

Coaching your team can sometimes be a tough job. In this book, we've already given you a lot to think about and work on. For those of you hungry for more, we've added this little appendix.

Here, we are going to take the concept of coaching from a downward focus to an upward one. You can coach up the line... it's trickier because you are the one in a more subordinate role. However, don't for a minute think that the coaching tools we presented in this book can't be useful to you when you are dealing with your own leader and organization. You just have to finesse your coaching technique a bit before you begin to coach your boss.

Make no mistake, there is a major need for the coaching of bosses in organizations. Think back over the jobs you have held in your life. How many times have you known someone in a leadership position who should have made a major difference, but didn't... at least not the difference they could have made. All of us can recall bosses, teachers, perhaps even ministers, who could have made a major difference but for whatever reason, didn't.

We may have complained privately or we might have left a job because we knew our boss was in trouble, but we did not step forward to help them become the leader they could have been. Why?

Well, one reason is that many people feel it would be "out of bounds" to even think that they could coach their boss. From early on, we are all taught to respect those in authority and not to question them: parents, teachers, sports coaches, and especially, bosses. Most people think that it is beyond the scope of their job to offer advice or guidance to their immediate leader. They might think that their boss would get upset at having his or her decisions and strategies questioned. And, these people might be right. That's why coaching your boss can be tricky. But, often, if coached with care, a boss can learn to really appreciate the coaching you give them and even reward you for it. It's up to you to decide if you want to take on the job.

In an age where downsizing is rampant, fear of losing one's job keeps many who could coach their boss on the sidelines. Coaching the boss can be risky. But, in good times and bad, coaching can be helpful at all levels of the organization.

If you, as a leader, have resolved yourself to using a coaching approach to leadership, the challenge is to help those below you and those above you to achieve their greatest potential. If we expect our direct reports to provide us uncensored information, unbiased advice and loyal support during tough

Appendix A:
Coaching Your Boss

times, then we must cultivate a culture that encourages them to do so. Likewise, if we want to be of the greatest service to our boss, we must provide timely advice and realistic options when their professional future (or that of the organization) is on the line.

Let's first examine how to coach your boss regarding your performance.

♦ If your boss isn't a coach, you may have to take up the gauntlet. You have to let him or her know that you want to be coached.

♦ Open a dialogue for trust between you and your boss.

♦ Let your boss know that you respect their position in the organizational hierarchy and that you would like to learn from them. However, you yourself need to realize that you are not subservient to your boss. We are all equals in life.

♦ Clarify expectations. Your boss isn't a mind reader and neither are you. Your boss can't know what it takes for you to do your job, what you need and what you want. You can't know what your boss wants from you unless you ask. Don't assume.

Having looked at coaching regarding your performance, let's briefly look at some situations when you may want to coach your boss regarding others in the organization.

♦ Your boss is micromanaging instead of macro-thinking.

♦ Your boss is making so many changes so quickly that people don't know where to focus their attention.

♦ Your boss is so focused on what people do wrong that people do exactly what is required – nothing more.

♦ Your boss's relationship with his boss is so contentious that it results in fewer resources or greater oversight and control for your team and other teams in the organization.

You will be able to add many other occasions where coaching your boss is appropriate. But always, always make sure the boss is receptive to coaching. Remember, the definition of "to be coached" – to take someone from where they are to where they... not you... want to be). No matter how great your coaching skills, trying to coach your boss in a direction the boss does not want to go (no matter what the reason) at best will frustrate you, and at worst could mean a career-shortening move.

Appendix A:
Coaching Your Boss

To coach your boss effectively, go back to Chapter 3 and review the difference between "confrontational" and "self" awareness. When you confront your boss, your communication skills are crucial. Speak softly, even tentatively. Use a questioning approach when appropriate. Remember, a major goal when coaching your boss is to move the boss from "confrontational" awareness to "self" awareness (ownership) for the effect the boss's actions or inactions are having.

In summary, whether you are coaching your boss regarding your own performance or how the boss can be more effective with others in the organization, there are some key ideas to keep in mind.

First, your relationship with your boss is everything. The strength of that relationship will determine how effectively you can coach her or him.

Second, displaying confidence in your boss will strengthen your relationship with your boss. In turn, you will find your boss displaying more confidence in you.

Third, sharing information with your boss makes the boss's job easier, builds the boss's trust in you and enhances the relationship between the two of you.

Finally, if you decide to coach your boss, it would be a good idea to go back and read the section on Relational Intelligence

(RQ) again. A focus on long-term, win/win relationships is always important whether you are coaching your boss... or your own winning team.

Appendix B

Coaches' Quotes

Great teamwork is the only way we create the breakthroughs that define our careers.

– Pat Riley

The measure of who we are is what we do with what we have.

– Vince Lombardi

My responsibility is getting all my players playing for the name on the front of the jersey, not the one on the back.

– author unknown (although lots of coaches use it)

It's so hard when you have to, but so easy when you want to.

– author unknown

Those who have invested the most are the last to surrender.

– author unknown

There is no obstacle that is too small to stumble over or too large to overcome.

– James Perry

Most coaches would say put this game behind you; but I don't want you to do that. I want you to remember how you feel right now every time you step out on that court to play. I want you to remember tonight whenever you see a loose ball or every time you feel tired and don't think you can make it. I want you to remember how you feel tonight because I never want to feel this way again.

– Jamey McRorie (High School Coach)

Imagination is more important than knowledge.

– Albert Einstein

Basketball is like photography, if you don't focus, all you have is the negative.

– Dan Frisby

A tough day at the office is even tougher when your OFFICE contains spectator seating.

– author unknown

Appendix B:
Coaches' Quotes

Extra discipline makes up for a lack of talent and a lack of discipline quickly siphons away extra talent, that's why it's frequently the most disciplined rather than the most gifted who rise to the top.

— author unknown

People need to know what you stand for, AND what you won't stand for.

— author unknown

When you have the attitude of a champion, you see adversity as your training partner.

— Colin Gillen

Teamwork: The fuel that produces uncommon results in common people.

— anonymous

If I was given eight hours to chop down a tree, I would spend seven hours sharpening my axe.

— Abraham Lincoln

Perception is reality. Remember it is not what you say or how you say it, but rather what is heard that is important.

– Ian Gray

Remember this, the choices you make in life, make you.

– John Wooden

What to do with a mistake – recognize it, admit it, learn from it, forget it.

– Dean Smith

If you think small things don't matter, think of the last game you lost by one point.

– author unknown

Coaches who can outline plays on a blackboard are a dime a dozen. The one's who win get inside their players and motivate.

– Vince Lombardi

Champions never complain, they are too busy getting better.

– author unknown

Appendix B:
Coaches' Quotes

It's not the hours you put in, it's what you put in the hours.

– author unknown

We are what we repeatedly do. Excellence then is not an act, but a habit.

– Aristotle

Keep it simple, when you get too complex you forget the obvious.

– Al Maguire

There are two kinds of people, those who do the work and those who take the credit. Try to be in the first group... there is less competition there.

– Indira Ghandi

The only difference between me and General Custer is that he didn't have to watch the games the next day.

– coach after losing in a humiliating defeat

90% of the game is played above the shoulders.

– Jim Geddes

The only important shot you take is the next one. Because not matter how hard you try, that is the only one you can still have an effect on.

— Jason Bumblis

It doesn't matter who scores the points, it's who can get the ball to the scorer.

— Larry Bird

Great efforts spring naturally from great attitude.

— Pat Riley

What the mind can conceive and believe, it can achieve.

— Napolean Hill

ABOUT THE AUTHOR

Richard C. Huseman, Ph.D.
rhuseman@give-to-get.com

Dick Huseman serves as an executive coach, keynote speaker, and consultant. He has had a variety of experiences in business school settings, serving as professor, department head, and dean. Working with companies like AT&T, Coca Cola, ExxonMobil, Adventist Health System and IBM, his focus has been in the areas of knowledge management, change management, and most importantly, relationship management.

Dick has co-authored nine books, including his most recent work, *Give-To-Get Leadership: The Secret of the Hidden Paycheck* (2002), as well as its precursor, *Managing The Equity Factor* (1989), which has been translated into Russian, German, Chinese, Portuguese, and Greek. **The Leader As Coach: How To Coach A Winning Team** is the culmination of 20 years of research and observation as to the true explanation of organizational performance and productivity – coaching in relationships.

The Leader As Coach

SPEAKING &
TRAINING PROGRAMS

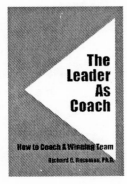

The Leader As Coach

How to Coach A Winning Team

Richard G. Huseman, Ph.D.

The Leader As Coach:
How To Coach A Winning Team

It doesn't matter whether you are on the team that's just won the Super Bowl, the World Series, or an Olympic gold medal – or your business team has been ranked number one in the company or you've just won a big government contract – there is nothing like the feeling of winning... unless it's the feeling you get **Coaching A Winning Team**.

The **Coaching A Winning Team** executive program series shows leaders what they can do to tap their employees' desire to win at work and bring about untold levels of effort and performance.

In reality, leadership isn't so much about the "leader" – it's about the relationship between the *leader* and the *people being led*. It is by focusing on this relationship that leaders can discover the secret of how to get a team to perform at their best and unlock broader and deeper levels of performance and profit. Then they, too, can find themselves **Leading A Winning Team**.

Coaching A Winning Team can be presented in a keynote, half-day or full-day seminar format. Each format can be specifically tailored and customized to meet the needs and environment of the hosting organization. Half and full day programs are highly interactive and include opportunities for self-assessment as well as several group exercises.

PRODUCTS

The Coaching Playbook

The Coaching Playbook is an individually tailored report generated for a manager/leader based on anonymous feedback gathered from their employees. It assesses how employees perceive their organization, their job, and especially their immediate manager.

Specifically, The Coaching Playbook offers managers/leaders feedback as to what "currencies," in addition to pay, are most important to their employees and the extent to which their employees feel they actually receive these other currencies.

Going far beyond 360° feedback, The Coaching Playbook then links what employees want from their work to several key managerial strategies that the manager/leader can implement on a day-to-day basis. Using these strategies, managers/leaders can give employees what they want from work and, in return, get the high performance and profit needed for success.

Coaching Playbook applications include:

- ♦ Supporting managers/leaders who are in challenging job assignments and want to be more effective with their teams.

- ♦ Securing real on-the-job data to compliment existing training programs.

- ♦ Providing content for coaching and feedback programs for managers/leaders.

INTERPERSONAL **C**OMMUNICATION **S**TYLE **S**URVEY	We all have a major strength as a communicator – do you know what yours is? Do you know how to leverage your communication strength when you interact with others? The Communication Style Survey is a self-assessment instrument designed to identify your major strength as a communicator and how you can effectively use that strength to your advantage.
PERSONAL **P**REFERENCES **I**NVENTORY	How do you really react to change? Is it in times of turbulence and transition or periods of stability and calm that you perform your best? The **Personal Preferences Inventory** is a self-assessment instrument that measures how you approach change on five key dimensions. You will not only gain insight into your own personal reactions to change but you will also discover how you can be more effective with your work team during periods of turbulence and major transition.

The Leader As Coach

PUBLICATIONS

The Secret of
THE HIDDEN PAYCHECK
Richard C. Huseman, Ph.D
Merwyn A. Hayes, Ph.D.

Give-To-Get Leadership:
The Secret of the Hidden Paycheck

Give-To-Get Leadership: The Secret of the Hidden Paycheck states that in an era of ruthless downsizing and merger, corporate loyalty is a thing of the past. Employees have too often gotten the short end of the stick from their employers and no longer believe that they are valued by their organizations. As such, corporate leaders at every level are facing the challenge of how to re-engage their employees and motivate them to higher levels of performance.

Leadership is a double-edged sword. The number one reason people say they are unhappy at work and quit their jobs..."I can't stand my manager/leader." However, the number one reason people stay at their jobs and perform well at work... "I have a great relationship with my manager/leader." How employees perceive their immediate manager/leader, be it the CEO or a front-line supervisor, determines whether employees perform at their best or at their worst (or maybe, not at all).

The book, **Give-To-Get Leadership: The Secret of the Hidden Paycheck**, outlines several strategies that enable leaders to give employees, in addition to pay, many of the other "currencies" employees really want from their work. When employees are paid these currencies, they are increasingly motivated to give the extra effort needed to generate high performance and profit.

Individual copies of
Give-To-Get Leadership: The Secret of the Hidden Paycheck
are available on Amazon.com for $22.95.

For multiple copies, please visit our website at www.give-to-get.com and inquire about our quantity discount plans.

Printed in the United States
1277700006B/1-108

9 780971 226029